Keto Chaffle Special Recipes

Enjoy Your Day with These Tasty Chaffle Dishes

Imogene Cook

TABLE OF CONTENTS

HOW TO MAKE CHAFFLES? 6

CHAFFLESS WITH KETO ICE CREAM 9

CHAFFLE TACOS 11

CHICKEN PARMESAN CHAFFLE 14

BROCCOLI AND CHEESE CHAFFLE 16

SIMPLE CORNBREAD CHAFFLE 18

TUNA CHAFFLES 20

GARLIC CHAFFLE STICKS 22

FRIED PICKLE CHAFFLE STICKS 24

SPICY JALAPENO POPPER CHAFFLESS 26

EGGNOG CHAFFLESS 28

BEEF MEATZA CHAFFLE 30

CHICKEN JALAPENO CHAFFLE 32

LAMB CHOPS ON CHAFFLE 34

CHICKEN PARMESAN CHAFFLES 36

PORK TZATZIKI CHAFFLE 38

MEDITERRANEAN LAMB KEBABS ON CHAFFLE 40

CREAMY BACON SALAD ON A CHAFFLE 42

BEEF AND SOUR CREAM CHAFFLE 44

PORK LOIN CHAFFLE SANDWICH 47

BEEF CHAFFLE TOWER 49

TURKEY BBQ SAUCE CHAFFLE 51

BEEF CHAFFLE SANDWICH RECIPE 53

KETO CHAFFLE BREAKFAST SANDWICH 55

CINNAMON ROLL KETO CHAFFLES 57

CHOCOLATE CHIP CHAFFLE KETO RECIPE 59

PUMPKIN CHOCOLATE CHIP CHAFFLES 61

CHEESY GARLIC CHAFFLE BREAD RECIPE 63

BEST KETO PIZZA CHAFFLE 65

EASY KETO CHAFFLE SAUSAGE GRAVY RECIPE 67

FUDGY CHOCOLATE CHAFFLES...70

MOUTHWATERING BLUEBERRY CHAFFLES..72

OPEN-FACED FRENCH DIP KETO CHAFFLE SANDWICH 74

KETO CHAFFLE TACO SHELLS 76

PEANUT BUTTER CHOCOLATE CHIP CHAFFLE 78

MINI KETO PIZZA CHAFFLE RECIPE...80

MAPLE PUMPKIN KETO CHAFFLE RECIPE...82

GARLIC BREAD CHAFFLES...84

BASIC KETO LOW CARB CHAFFLE RECIPE 86

KETO PROTEIN CHAFFLE..88

GARLIC MAYO VEGAN CHAFFLES 90

BROCCOLI CHAFFLE 92

CELERY AND COTTAGE CHEESE CHAFFLE 94

DIRECTIONS: 95

LETTUCE CHAFFLE SANDWICH..96

COCOA CHAFFLES WITH COCONUT CREAM 98

SHRIMP AVOCADO CHAFFLE SANDWICH 100

CUBAN PORK SANDWICH..103

KETO CHOCOLATE CHAFFLES 105

TUNA SALAD CHAFFLES..107

KETO PIZZA CHAFFLE..109

How to Make Chaffles?

Equipment and Ingredients Discussed

Making chaffles requires five simple steps and nothing more than a waffle maker for flat chaffles and a waffle bowl maker for chaffle bowls.

To make chaffles, you will need two necessary ingredients –eggs and cheese. My preferred cheeses are cheddar cheese or mozzarella cheese. These melt quickly, making them the go-to for most recipes. Meanwhile, always ensure that your cheeses are finely grated or thinly sliced for use.

Now, to make a standard chaffle:

First, preheat your waffle maker until adequately hot.

Meanwhile, in a bowl, mix the egg with cheese on hand until well combined.

Open the iron, pour in a quarter or half of the mixture, and close.

Cook the chaffle for 5 to 7 minutes or until it is crispy.

Transfer the chaffle to a plate and allow cooling before serving.

11 Tips to Make Chaffles

My surefire ways to turn out the crispiest of chaffles:

Preheat Well: Yes! It sounds obvious to preheat the waffle iron before usage. However, preheating the iron moderately

will not get your chaffles as crispy as you will like. The best way to preheat before cooking is to ensure that the iron is very hot.

Not-So-Cheesy: Will you prefer to have your chaffles less cheesy? Then use mozzarella cheese.

Not-So Eggy: If you aren't comfortable with the smell of eggs in your chaffles, try using egg whites instead of egg yolks or whole eggs.

To Shred or to Slice: Many recipes call for shredded cheese when making chaffles, but I find sliced cheeses to offer crispier pieces. While I stick with mostly shredded cheese for convenience's sake, be at ease to use sliced cheese in the same quantity. When using sliced cheeses, arrange two to four pieces in the waffle iron, top with the beaten eggs, and some slices of the cheese. Cover and cook until crispy.

Shallower Irons: For better crisps on your chaffles, use shallower waffle irons as they cook easier and faster.

Layering: Don't fill up the waffle iron with too much batter. Work between a quarter and a half cup of total ingredients per batch for correctly done chaffles.

Patience: It is a virtue even when making chaffles. For the best results, allow the chaffles to sit in the iron for 5 to 7 minutes before serving.

No Peeking: 7 minutes isn't too much of a time to wait for the outcome of your chaffles, in my opinion.

Opening the iron and checking on the chaffle before

it is done stands you a worse chance of ruining it.

Crispy Cooling: For better crisp, I find that allowing the chaffles to cool further after they are transferred to a plate aids a lot.

Easy Cleaning: For the best cleanup, wet a paper towel and wipe the inner parts of the iron clean while still warm. Kindly note that the iron should be warm but not hot!

Brush It: Also, use a clean toothbrush to clean between the iron's teeth for a thorough cleanup. You may also use a dry, rough sponge to clean the iron while it is still warm.

Chaffless with Keto Ice Cream

Preparation Time: 10 minutes

Cooking Time: 14 minutes

Servings: 2

Ingredients:

- one egg, beaten
- ½ cup finely grated mozzarella cheese
- ¼ cup almond flour
- 2 tbsp Swerve confectioner's sugar
- 1/8 tsp xanthan gum
- Low-carb ice cream (flavor of your choice) for serving

Directions:

1. Preheat the waffle iron.
2. In a medium bowl, mix all the ingredients except the ice cream.
3. Open the iron and add half of the mixture. Close and cook until crispy, 7 minutes.

4. Transfer the chaffle to a plate and make the second one with the remaining batter.

5. On each chaffle, add a scoop of low carb ice cream, fold into half-moons and enjoy.

Nutrition:

Calories: 89 Cal Total Fat: 6.48 g Saturated Fat: 0 g Cholesterol:

0 mg Sodium: 0 mg Total Carbs: 1.37 g Fibre: 0 g Sugar: 0 g Protein: 5.91 g

Chaffle Tacos

Preparation Time: 10 minutes

Cooking Time: 15 minutes

Servings: 4

Ingredients:

Chaffle:

- 2 tbsp coconut flour
- 3 eggs (beaten)
- ½ cup shredded mozzarella cheese
- ½ cup shredded cheddar cheese
- A pinch of salt
- ½ tsp oregano

Taco Filling:

- 1 garlic clove (minced)
- 1 small onion (finely chopped)
- ½ pound ground beef
- 1 tsp olive oil
- 1 tsp cumin

- ½ tsp Italian seasoning
- 1 tsp paprika
- 1 tsp chili powder
- 1 roma tomato (diced)
- 1 green bell pepper (diced)
- 4 tbsp sour cream
- 1 tbsp chopped green onions

Directions:

1. Plug the waffle maker to preheat it and spray it with a non-stick cooking spray.
2. In a mixing bowl, combine the mozzarella cheese, cheddar, coconut flour, salt, and oregano. Add the eggs and mix until the ingredients are well combined.
3. Fill the waffle maker with an appropriate amount of the batter. Spread the mixture to the edges to cover all the holes on the waffle maker.
4. Close the waffle maker and cook for about 5 minutes or according to the waffle maker's settings.
5. After the cooking cycle, use a plastic or silicone utensil to remove the chaffle from the waffle maker. Set aside.
6. Repeat steps 3 to 5 until you have cooked all the batter into chaffless.
7. Heat a large skillet over medium to high heat.

8. Transfer the beef to a paper towel-lined plate to drain and wipe the skillet clean.
9. Add the olive oil and leave it to get hot.
10. Add the onions and garlic and saute for 3-4 minutes or until the onion is translucent, stirring often.
11. Add the diced tomatoes and green pepper—Cook for 1 minute.
12. Add the browned ground beef. Stir in the cumin, paprika, chilli powder, and Italian seasoning.
13. Reduce the heat and cook on low for about 8 minutes, often stirring to prevent burning.
14. Remove the skillet from heat.
15. Scoop the taco mixture into the chaffless and top with chopped green onion and sour cream.
16. Enjoy.

Nutrition:

Servings: 4 Amount per serving Calories 321 % Daily Value Total Fat 17.5g 22% Saturated Fat 8.5g 43% Cholesterol 196mg 65% Sodium 266mg 12% Total Carbohydrate 12.6g 5% Dietary Fiber 4.4g 16% Total Sugars 4.5g Protein 28.6g Vitamin D 13mcg 66% Calcium 156mg 12% Iron 13mg 74% Potassium 533mg 11%

Chicken Parmesan Chaffle

Preparation Time: 5 minutes

Cooking Time: 13 minutes

Servings: 2

Ingredients:

- 1 egg (beaten)
- ½ cup shredded chicken
- 2 tbsp shredded parmesan cheese
- 1/3 cup shredded mozzarella cheese
- ¼ tsp garlic powder
- ¼ tsp onion powder
- 2 tbsp marinara sauce
- 1 tsp Italian seasoning

Garnish:

- 1 tbsp chopped green onions

Directions:

1. Plug the waffle maker to preheat it and spray it with a non-stick cooking spray.
2. In a mixing bowl, combine the mozzarella cheese, shredded chicken, Italian seasoning, onion powder, and garlic powder. Add the egg and mix until the ingredients

are well combined.

3. Pour half of the batter into the waffle maker and spread out the mixture to the edges to cover all the holes on the waffle maker.
4. Close the waffle maker and cook for about 4 minutes or according to your waffle maker's settings.
5. Meanwhile, preheat your oven to 400°F and line a baking sheet with parchment paper.
6. After the cooking cycle, use a plastic or silicone utensil to remove the chaffle from the waffle maker.
7. Repeat 3, 4 and 6 to make the second chaffle.
8. Spread marinara sauce over the surface of both chaffless and sprinkle the parmesan cheese over the chaffless.
9. Arrange the chaffless into the baking sheet and place them in the oven—Bake for about 5 minutes or until the cheese melts.
10. Remove the chaffless from the oven and let them cool for a few minutes.
11. Serve and top with chopped green onion.

Nutrition:

Servings: 2 Amount per serving Calories 144 % Daily Value Total Fat 6.7g 9% Saturated Fat 2.7g 14% Cholesterol 118mg 39% Sodium 212mg 9% Total Carbohydrate 3.7g 1% Dietary Fiber0.5g 2% Total Sugars 2g Protein 16.9g Vitamin D 8mcg 39% Calcium 89mg 7% Iron 1mg 5% Potassium 160mg 3%

Broccoli and Cheese Chaffle

Preparation Time: 5 minutes

Cooking Time: 15 minutes

Servings: 1

Ingredients:

- 1/3 cup broccoli (finely chopped)
- ½ tsp oregano
- 1/8 tsp salt or to taste
- 1/8 tsp ground black pepper or to taste
- ½ tsp garlic powder
- ½ tsp onion powder
- 1 egg (beaten)
- 4 tbsp shredded cheddar cheese

Directions:

1. Plug the waffle maker to preheat it and spray it with a non-stick cooking spray.
2. In a mixing bowl, combine the cheese, oregano, pepper, garlic, salt, and onion. Add the egg and mix until the

ingredients are well combined.

3. Fold in the chopped broccoli.
4. Pour an appropriate amount of the batter into your waffle maker and spread out the mixture to the edges to cover all the holes on the waffle maker.
5. Cook time may vary in some waffle makers.
6. After the cooking cycle, use a silicone or plastic utensil to remove the chaffle from the waffle maker.
7. Repeat steps 4 to 6 until you have cooked all the batter into chaffless.
8. Serve and top with sour cream as desired.

Nutrition:

Servings: 1 Amount per serving Calories 198% Daily Value Total Fat 13.9g 18% Saturated Fat 7.3g 37% Cholesterol 193mg 64% Sodium 539mg 23% Total Carbohydrate 5.2g 2% Dietary Fiber 1.3g 5% Total Sugars 1.8g Protein 13.9g Vitamin D 19mcg 94% Calcium 259mg 20% Iron 2mg 10% Potassium 222mg 5%

Simple Cornbread Chaffle

Preparation Time: 4 minutes

Cooking Time: 10 minutes

Servings: 4

Ingredients:

- 4 eggs
- 1 cup cheddar cheese, shredded
- 8 slices jalapeno, optional
- 1 tsp red hot sauce
- ¼ tsp low carb corn extract
- Pinch salt

Directions:

1. Preheat the waffle maker.
2. Crack the eggs in a small bowl and whip.
3. Add all the other ingredients and mix thoroughly.
4. Add a pinch of shredded cheese to the hot waffle maker. Cook for 30 seconds.
5. Pour half the egg mixture to the preheated waffle maker.

6. Cook for 5 minutes.

7. Remove, allow to cool, and enjoy.

Nutrition:

Calories: 155 Cal Total Fat: 12 g Saturated Fat: 0 g Cholesterol: 0 mg Sodium: 0 mg Total Carbs: 1.2 g Fibre: 0 g Sugar: 0 g Protein: 10 g

Tuna Chaffles

Preparation Time: 5 minutes

Cooking Time: 8 minutes

Servings: 2

Ingredients:

- one packet Tuna, drained
- ½ cup mozzarella cheese
- One egg
- A pinch of salt

Directions:

1. Preheat, the waffle maker
2. Whip the egg in a small mixing bowl.
3. Add the tuna, cheese, and season with the salt. Mix well.
4. For a crispy crust, add a teaspoon of shredded cheese to the waffle maker and cook for 30 seconds.
5. Pour half the mixture to the mini waffle maker and cook for 4 minutes.

6. Remove it and repeat the process with the remaining tuna chaffle mixture.
7. Once ready, remove and enjoy warm.

Nutrition:

Calories: 650 Cal Total Fat: 39 g Saturated Fat: 0 g Cholesterol: 0mg Sodium: 0 mg Total Carbs: 6 g Fibre: 0 g Sugar: 0 g Protein: 63 g

Garlic Chaffle Sticks

Preparation Time: 10 minutes

Cooking Time: 15 minutes

Servings: 4

Ingredients:

- Two eggs
- 1 cup mozzarella cheese, grated
- 4 tbsp almond flour
- 1 tsp garlic powder
- 1 tsp oregano
- ½ teaspoon salt

Toppings:

- 4 tbsp butter, unsalted softened
- ½ tsp garlic powder
- ½ cup mozzarella cheese, grated

Directions:

1. Preheat your waffle maker.
2. Whisk the eggs in a small bowl.
3. Add the almond flour, mozzarella, oregano, garlic powder, and salt. Mix well.

4. Spoon half the egg mixture into your waffle maker. Cook for 5 minutes and remove it.
5. Repeat the process with the remaining batter and cook for 5 minutes.
6. Remove from the waffle maker and cut into four strips out of each waffle.
7. Place the waffle sticks on a tray and preheat your grill.
8. Add the butter and garlic powder in a small mixing bowl. Mix properly.
9. Using a brush spread the garlic mixture over the sticks.
10. Sprinkle the shredded mozzarella over the sticks. Place under the grill for 3 minutes or until the cheese starts to melt and bubble.
11. Eat immediately!
12. Cheese is a significant ingredient when preparing chaffless. However, if you aren't a fan of cheese, there are many ways to get around it. Although they may not taste quite the same, almond milk, ricotta is a delicious alternative to cheese! It has the consistency of contemporary cheese and provides a flavorful alternative to dairy cheese in many recipes.

Nutrition: Calories: 109 Cal Total Fat: 19 g Saturated Fat: 0 g Cholesterol: 0mg Sodium: 0 mg Total Carbs: 7 g Fiber: 0 g Sugar: 0 g Protein: 27 g

Fried pickle chaffle sticks

Preparation Time: 5 minutes

Cooking Time: 15 minutes

Servings: 1

Ingredients:

- One egg
- 1/2 cup mozzarella cheese
- 1/4 cup pork panko
- 6-8 pickle slices, thinly sliced
- 1 tbsp pickle juice

Directions:

1. Mix all the ingredients, except the pickle slices, in a small bowl.
2. Use a paper towel to blot out excess liquid from the pickle slices.
3. Add a thin layer of the mixture to a preheated waffle iron.
4. Add some pickle slices before adding another thin layer of the mixture.

5. Close the waffle maker's lid and allow the mixture to cook for 4 minutes.
6. Optional: combine hot sauce with ranch to create a great-tasting dip.

Nutrition:

Calories: 465 Cal Total Fat: 22.7 g Saturated Fat: 0 g Cholesterol: 0 mg Sodium: 0 mg Total Carbs: 3.3 g Fibre: 0 g Sugar: 0 g Protein: 59.2 g

Spicy jalapeno popper chaffless

Preparation Time: 5 minutes

Cooking Time: 10 minutes

Servings: 1

Ingredients: for the chaffless:

- One egg
- 1 oz cream cheese, softened
- 1 cup cheddar cheese, shredded

For the toppings:

- 2 tbsp bacon bits
- 1/2 tbsp jalapenos

Directions:

1. Turn on the waffle maker. Preheat for up to 5 minutes.
2. Mix the chaffle Ingredients.
3. Pour the batter onto the waffle maker.
4. Cook the butter for 3-4 minutes until it's brown and crispy.

5. Sprinkle bacon bits and a few jalapeno slices as toppings.

Nutrition:

Calories: 231 Cal Total Fat: 18 g Saturated Fat: 0 g Cholesterol: 0 mg Sodium: 0 mg Total Carbs: 2 g Fibre: 0 g Sugar: 0 g Protein: 13 g

Eggnog chaffless

Preparation Time: 5 minutes

Cooking Time: 15 minutes

Servings: 1

Ingredients:

- One egg, separated
- One egg yolk
- 1/2 cup mozzarella cheese, shredded
- 1/2 tsp spiced rum
- 1 tsp vanilla extract
- 1/4 tsp nutmeg, dried
- A dash of cinnamon
- 1 tsp coconut flour

For the icing:

- 2 tbsp cream cheese
- 1 tbsp powdered sweetener
- 2 tsp rum or rum extract

Directions:

1. Preheat the mini waffle maker.
2. Mix egg yolk in a small bowl until smooth.
3. Add the coconut flour, cinnamon, and nutmeg. Mix well.
4. In another bowl, mix rum, egg white, and vanilla. Whisk until well combined.
5. Throw in the yolk mixture with the egg white mixture. You should be able to form a thin batter.
6. Add the mozzarella cheese and combine with the mixture.
7. Separate the batter into two batches. Put 1/2 of the mixture into the waffle maker and let it cook for 6 minutes until it's reliable.
8. Repeat until you've used up the remaining batter.
9. In a separate bowl, mix all the icing ingredients.
10. Top the cooked chaffless with the icing, or you can use this as a dip.

Nutrition:

Calories: 266 Cal Total Fat: 23 g Saturated Fat: 0 g Cholesterol: 0mg Sodium: 0 mg Total Carbs: 2 g Fiber: 0 g Sugar: 0 g Protein: 13 g

Beef Meatza Chaffle

Preparation time: 10 minutes

Cooking Time:15 Minutes

Servings: 2

Ingredients:

- Meatza chaffle batter
- ½ pound ground beef
- 4 eggs
- 2 cups grated cheddar cheese
- Salt and pepper to taste
- 1 teaspoon Italian seasoning
- 2 tablespoons tomato sauce

Other

- 2 tablespoons cooking spray to brush the waffle maker
- ¼ cup tomato sauce for serving
- 2 tablespoons freshly chopped basil for serving

Directions:

1. Preheat the waffle maker.
2. Add the ground beef, eggs, grated cheddar cheese, salt and pepper, Italian seasoning and tomato sauce to a bowl.
3. Mix until everything is fully combined.
4. Brush the heated waffle maker with cooking spray and add a few tablespoons of the batter.
5. Close the lid and cook for about 7–10 minutes depending on your waffle maker.
6. Serve with tomato sauce and freshly chopped basil on top.

Nutrition:

Calories 4, fat 34.6 g, carbs 2.5 g, sugar 1.7 g, Protein 36.5 g, sodium 581 mg

Chicken Jalapeno Chaffle

Preparation time: 10 minutes

Cooking Time:8–10 Minutes

Servings: 2

Ingredients:

Batter

- ½ pound ground chicken
- 4 eggs
- 1 cup grated mozzarella cheese
- 2 tablespoons sour cream
- 1 green jalapeno, chopped
- Salt and pepper to taste
- 1 teaspoon dried oregano
- ½ teaspoon dried garlic

Other

- 2 tablespoons butter to brush the waffle maker
- ¼ cup sour cream to garnish
- 1 green jalapeno, diced, to garnish

Directions:

1. Preheat the waffle maker.
2. Add the ground chicken, eggs, mozzarella cheese, sour cream, chopped jalapeno, salt and pepper, dried oregano and dried garlic to a bowl.
3. Mix everything until batter forms.
4. Brush the heated waffle maker with butter and add a few tablespoons of the batter.
5. Close the lid and cook for about 8–10 minutes depending on your waffle maker.
6. Serve with a tablespoon of sour cream and sliced jalapeno on top.

Nutrition:

Calories 284, fat 19.4 g, carbs 2.2 g, sugar 0.6 g, Protein 24.g, sodium 204 mg

Lamb Chops On Chaffle

Preparation time: 10 minutes

Cooking Time:15 Minutes

Servings: 2

Ingredients:

- 4 eggs
- 2 cups grated mozzarella cheese
- Salt and pepper to taste
- 1 teaspoon garlic powder
- ¼ cup heavy cream
- 6 tablespoons almond flour
- 2 teaspoons baking powder
- Lamb chops
- 2 tablespoons herbed butter
- 1 pound lamb chops
- Salt and pepper to taste
- 1 teaspoon freshly chopped rosemary
- Other
- 2 tablespoons butter to brush the waffle maker
- 2 tablespoons freshly chopped parsley for garnish

Directions:

1. Preheat the waffle maker.
2. Add the eggs, mozzarella cheese, salt and pepper, garlic powder, heavy cream, almond flour and baking powder to a bowl.
3. Mix until combined.
4. Brush the heated waffle maker with butter and add a few tablespoons of the batter.
5. Close the lid and cook for about 7 minutes depending on your waffle maker.
6. Meanwhile, heat a nonstick frying pan and rub the lamb chops with herbed butter, salt and pepper, and freshly chopped rosemary.
7. Cook the lamb chops for about 3–4 minutes on each side.
8. Serve each chaffle with a few lamb chops and sprinkle on some freshly chopped parsley for a nice presentation.

Nutrition:

Calories 537, fat 37.3 g, carbs 5.5 g, sugar 0.6 g, Protein 44.3 g, sodium 328 mg

Chicken Parmesan Chaffles

Preparation time: 10 minutes

Cooking Time: 8 Minutes

Servings: 2

Ingredients:

1/3 cup chicken

1 egg

1/3 cup mozzarella cheese

1/4 tsp basil

1/4 garlic

2 tbsp tomato sauce

2 tbsp Mozarella cheese

Directions:

1. Heat up your Dash mini waffle maker.
2. In a small bowl, mix the egg, cooked chicken, basil, garlic, and Mozzarella Cheese.

3. Add 1/2 of the batter into your mini waffle maker and cook for 4 minutes. If they are still a bit uncooked, leave it cooking for another 2 minutes. Then cook the rest of the batter to make a second chaffle and then cook the third chaffle.
4. After cooking, remove from the pan and let sit for 2 minutes.
5. Top with 1-2 tablespoons sauce on each chicken parmesan chaffle. Then sprinkle 1-2 tablespoon mozzarella cheese.
6. Put chaffles in the oven or a toaster oven at 400 degrees and cook until the cheese is melted.

Nutrition:

(per serving): Calories: 185kcal ; Carbohydrates:2g ; Protein: 14g; Fat:13g; Saturated Fat:6g; Cholesterol:122mg; Sodium:254mg; Potassium: 66mg ; Sugar: 1g ; Vitamin A: 3IU ; Calcium: 181mg ; Iron: 1mg

Pork Tzatziki Chaffle

Preparation time: 10 minutes

Cooking Time:25 Minutes

Servings: 2

Ingredients:

- 4 eggs
- 2 cups grated provolone cheese
- Salt and pepper to taste
- 1 teaspoon dried rosemary
- 1 teaspoon dried oregano
- Pork loin
- 2 tablespoons olive oil
- 1 pound pork tenderloin
- Salt and pepper to taste
- Tzatziki sauce
- 1 cup sour cream
- Salt and pepper to taste
- 1 cucumber, peeled and diced
- 1 teaspoon garlic powder
- 1 teaspoon dried dill

Other

- 2 tablespoons butter to brush the waffle maker

Directions:

1. Preheat the waffle maker.
2. Add the eggs, grated provolone cheese, dried rosemary, and dried oregano to a bowl. Season with salt and pepper to taste.
3. Mix until combined.
4. Brush the heated waffle maker with butter and add a few tablespoons of the batter.
5. Close the lid and cook for about 7 minutes depending on your waffle maker.
6. Meanwhile, heat the olive oil in a nonstick frying pan. Generously season the pork tenderloin with salt and pepper and cook it for about 7 minutes on each side.
7. Mix the sour cream, salt and pepper, diced cucumber, garlic powder and dried dill in a bowl.
8. Serve each chaffle with a few tablespoons of tzatziki sauce and slices of pork tenderloin.

Nutrition:

Calories 700, fat 50.g, carbs 6 g, sugar 1.5 g, Protein 54.4 g, sodium 777 mg

Mediterranean Lamb Kebabs on Chaffle

Preparation time: 10 minutes

Cooking Time:15 Minutes

Servings: 2

Ingredients:

- 4 eggs
- 2 cups grated mozzarella cheese
- Salt and pepper to taste
- 1 teaspoon garlic powder
- ¼ cup Greek yogurt
- ½ cup coconut flour
- 2 teaspoons baking powder
- Lamb kebabs
- 1 pound ground lamb meat
- Salt and pepper to taste
- 1 egg
- 2 tablespoons almond flour
- 1 spring onion, finely chopped
- ½ teaspoon dried garlic
- 2 tablespoons olive oil

Other

- 2 tablespoons butter to brush the waffle maker

- ¼ cup sour cream for serving
- 4 sprigs of fresh dill for garnish

Directions:

1. Preheat the waffle maker.
2. Add the eggs, mozzarella cheese, salt and pepper, garlic powder, Greek yogurt, coconut flour and baking powder to a bowl.
3. Mix until combined.
4. Brush the heated waffle maker with butter and add a few tablespoons of the batter.
5. Close the lid and cook for about 7 minutes depending on your waffle maker.
6. Meanwhile, add the ground lamb, salt and pepper, egg, almond flour, chopped spring onion, and dried garlic to a bowl. Mix and
7. form medium-sized kebabs.
8. Impale each kebab on a skewer. Heat the olive oil in a frying pan.
9. Cook the lamb kebabs for about 3 minutes on each side.
10. Serve each chaffle with a tablespoon of sour cream and one or two lamb kebabs. Decorate with fresh dill.

Nutrition: Calories 679, fat 49.9 g, carbs 15.8 g, sugar 0.8 g, Protein 42.6 g, sodium 302 mg

Creamy Bacon Salad on A Chaffle

Preparation time: 10 minutes

Cooking Time:15 Minutes

Servings: 2

Ingredients:

- 4 eggs
- 1½ cups grated mozzarella cheese
- ½ cup parmesan cheese
- Salt and pepper to taste
- 1 teaspoon dried oregano
- ¼ cup almond flour
- 2 teaspoons baking powder
- Bacon salad
- ½ pound cooked bacon
- 1 cup cream cheese
- 1 teaspoon dried oregano
- 1 teaspoon dried basil
- 1 teaspoon dried rosemary
- 2 tablespoons lemon juice

Other

- 2 tablespoons butter to brush the waffle maker
- 2 spring onions, finely chopped, for serving

Directions:

1. Preheat the waffle maker.
2. Add the eggs, mozzarella cheese, parmesan cheese, salt and
3. pepper, dried oregano, almond flour and baking powder to a bowl.
4. Mix until combined.
5. Brush the heated waffle maker with butter and add a few tablespoons of the batter.
6. Close the lid and cook for about 7 minutes depending on your waffle maker.
7. Meanwhile, chop the cooked bacon into smaller pieces and place them in a bowl with the cream cheese. Season with dried oregano, dried basil, dried rosemary and lemon juice.
8. Mix until combined and spread each chaffle with the creamy bacon salad.
9. To serve, sprinkle some freshly chopped spring onion on top.

Nutrition:

Calories 750, fat 62.5 g, carbs 7.7 g, sugar 0.8 g, Protein 40.3 g, sodium 1785 mg

Beef and Sour Cream Chaffle

Preparation time: 10 minutes

Cooking Time:15 Minutes

Servings: 2

Ingredients:

Batter

- 4 eggs
- 2 cups grated mozzarella cheese
- 3 tablespoons coconut flour
- 3 tablespoons almond flour
- 2 teaspoons baking powder
- Salt and pepper to taste
- 1 tablespoon freshly chopped parsley
- Seasoned beef
- 1 pound beef tenderloin
- Salt and pepper to taste
- 2 tablespoons olive oil
- 1 tablespoon Dijon mustard

Other

- 2 tablespoons olive oil to brush the waffle maker
- ¼ cup sour cream for garnish
- 2 tablespoons freshly chopped spring onion for garnish

Directions:

1. Preheat the waffle maker.
2. Add the eggs, grated mozzarella cheese, coconut flour, almond flour, baking powder, salt and pepper and freshly chopped parsley to a bowl.
3. Mix until just combined and batter forms.
4. Brush the heated waffle maker with olive oil and add a few tablespoons of the batter.
5. Close the lid and cook for about 7 minutes depending on your waffle maker.
6. Meanwhile, heat the olive oil in a nonstick pan over medium heat.
7. Season the beef tenderloin with salt and pepper and spread the whole piece of beef tenderloin with Dijon mustard.
8. Cook on each side for about 4–5 minutes.
9. Serve each chaffle with sour cream and slices of the cooked beef tenderloin.
10. Garnish with freshly chopped spring onion.

11. Serve and enjoy.

Nutrition:

Calories 543, fat 37 g, carbs 7.9 g, sugar 0.5 g, Protein 44.9 g, sodium 269 mg

Pork Loin Chaffle Sandwich

Preparation time: 10 minutes

Cooking Time:15 Minutes

Servings: 2

Ingredients:

- 4 eggs
- 1 cup grated mozzarella cheese
- 1 cup grated parmesan cheese
- Salt and pepper to taste
- 2 tablespoons cream cheese
- 6 tablespoons coconut flour
- 2 teaspoons baking powder
- Pork loin
- 2 tablespoons olive oil
- 1 pound pork loin
- Salt and pepper to taste
- 2 cloves garlic, minced
- 1 tablespoon freshly chopped thyme

Other

- 2 tablespoons cooking spray to brush the waffle maker
- 4 lettuce leaves for serving

- 4 slices of tomato for serving
- ¼ cup sugar-free mayonnaise for serving

Directions:

1. Preheat the waffle maker.
2. Add the eggs, mozzarella cheese, parmesan cheese, salt and pepper, cream cheese, coconut flour and baking powder to a bowl.
3. Mix until combined.
4. Brush the heated waffle maker with cooking spray and add a few tablespoons of the batter.
5. Close the lid and cook for about 7 minutes depending on your waffle maker.
6. Meanwhile, heat the olive oil in a nonstick frying pan and season the pork loin with salt and pepper, minced garlic and freshly chopped thyme.
7. Cook the pork loin for about 5–minutes on each side.
8. Cut each chaffle in half and add some mayonnaise, lettuce leaf, tomato slice and sliced pork loin on one half.
9. Cover the sandwich with the other chaffle half and serve.

Nutrition:

Calories 7 fat 52.7 g, carbs 11.3 g, sugar 0.8 g, Protein 47.4 g, sodium 513 mg

Beef Chaffle Tower

Preparation time: 10 minutes

Cooking Time:15 Minutes

Servings: 2

Ingredients:

Batter

- 4 eggs
- 2 cups grated mozzarella cheese
- Salt and pepper to taste
- 2 tablespoons almond flour
- 1 teaspoon Italian seasoning
- Beef
- 2 tablespoons butter
- 1 pound beef tenderloin
- Salt and pepper to taste
- 1 teaspoon chili flakes

Other

- 2 tablespoons cooking spray to brush the waffle maker

Directions:

1. Preheat the waffle maker.
2. Add the eggs, grated mozzarella cheese, salt and pepper, almond flour and Italian seasoning to a bowl.
3. Mix until everything is fully combined.
4. Brush the heated waffle maker with cooking spray and add a few tablespoons of the batter.
5. Close the lid and cook for about 7 minutes depending on your waffle maker.
6. Meanwhile, heat the butter in a nonstick frying pan and season the beef tenderloin with salt and pepper and chili flakes.
7. Cook the beef tenderloin for about 5–minutes on each side.
8. When serving, assemble the chaffle tower by placing one chaffle on a plate, a layer of diced beef tenderloin, another chaffle, another layer of beef, and so on until you finish with the chaffles and beef.
9. Serve and enjoy.

Nutrition:

Calories 412, fat 25 g, carbs 1.8 g, sugar 0.5 g, Protein 43.2 g, sodium 256 mg

Turkey Bbq Sauce Chaffle

Preparation time: 10 minutes

Cooking Time:8–10 Minutes

Servings: 2

Ingredients:

Batter

- ½ pound ground turkey meat
- 3 eggs
- 1 cup grated Swiss cheese
- ¼ cup cream cheese
- ¼ cup BBQ sauce
- 1 teaspoon dried oregano
- Salt and pepper to taste
- 2 cloves garlic, minced

Other

- 2 tablespoons butter to brush the waffle maker
- ¼ cup BBQ sauce for serving
- 2 tablespoons freshly chopped parsley for garnish
-

Directions:

1. Preheat the waffle maker.
2. Add the ground turkey, eggs, grated Swiss cheese, cream cheese, BBQ sauce, dried oregano, salt and pepper, and minced garlic to a bowl.
3. Mix everything until combined and batter forms.
4. Brush the heated waffle maker with butter and add a few tablespoons of the batter.
5. Close the lid and cook for about 8–10 minutes depending on your waffle maker.
6. Serve each chaffle with a tablespoon of BBQ sauce and a sprinkle of freshly chopped parsley.

Nutrition:

Calories 365, fat 23.g, carbs 13.7 g, sugar 8.8 g, Protein 23.5 g, sodium 595 mg

Beef Chaffle Sandwich Recipe

Preparation time: 10 minutes

Cooking Time:15 Minutes

Servings: 2

Ingredients:

Batter

- 3 eggs
- 2 cups grated mozzarella cheese
- ¼ cup cream cheese
- Salt and pepper to taste
- 1 teaspoon Italian seasoning
- Beef
- 2 tablespoons butter
- 1 pound beef tenderloin
- Salt and pepper to taste
- 2 teaspoons Dijon mustard
- 1 teaspoon dried paprika

Other

- 2 tablespoons cooking spray to brush the waffle maker
- 4 lettuce leaves for serving
- 4 tomato slices for serving
- 4 leaves fresh basil

Directions:

1. Preheat the waffle maker.
2. Add the eggs, grated mozzarella cheese, salt and pepper and Italian seasoning to a bowl.
3. Mix until combined and batter forms.
4. Brush the heated waffle maker with cooking spray and add a few tablespoons of the batter.
5. Close the lid and cook for about 7 minutes depending on your waffle maker.
6. Meanwhile, melt and heat the butter in a nonstick frying pan.
7. Season the beef loin with salt and pepper, brush it with Dijon mustard, and sprinkle some dried paprika on top.
8. Cook the beef on each side for about 5 minutes.
9. Thinly slice the beef and assemble the chaffle sandwiches.
10. Cut each chaffle in half and on one half place a lettuce leaf, tomato slice, basil leaf, and some sliced beef.
11. Cover with the other chaffle half and serve.

Nutrition:

Calories 477, fat 32.8g, carbs 2.3 g, sugar 0.9 g, Protein 42.2 g, sodium 299 mg

Keto Chaffle Breakfast Sandwich

Preparation time: 10 minutes

Cooking Time: 6 Minutes

Servings: 2

Ingredients:

- 1 egg
- 1/2 cup Monterey Jack Cheese
- 1 tablespoon almond flour
- 2 tablespoons butter

Directions:

1. In a small bowl, mix the egg, almond flour, and Monterey Jack Cheese.
2. Pour half of the batter into your mini waffle maker and cook for 3-4 minutes. Then cook the rest of the batter to make a second chaffle.
3. In a small pan, melt 2 tablespoons of butter. Add the chaffles and cook on each side for 2 minutes. Pressing down while they are cooking lightly on the top of them, so

they crisp up better.

4. Remove from the pan and let sit for 2 minutes.

Nutrition:

(per serving): Calories: 4kcal; Carbohydrates:2g; Protein: 21g; Fat:47g; Saturated Fat:27g; Cholesterol:274mg; Sodium:565mg; Potassium:106mg; Fiber: 1g; Sugar: 1g; Vitamin A: 1372IU; Calcium: 461mg; Iron: 1mg

Cinnamon Roll Keto Chaffles

Preparation time: 10 minutes

Cooking Time: 10 Minutes

Servings: 2

Ingredients:

- Cinnamon Roll Chaffle
- 1/2 cup mozzarella cheese
- 1 tablespoon almond flour
- 1/4 tsp baking powder
- 1 egg
- 1 tsp cinnamon
- 1 tsp Granulated Swerve
- Cinnamon roll swirl
- 1 tbsp butter
- 1 tsp cinnamon
- 2 tsp confectioners swerve
- Keto Cinnamon Roll Glaze
- 1 tablespoon butter
- 1 tablespoon cream cheese
- 1/4 tsp vanilla extract
- 2 tsp swerve confectioners

Directions:

1. Plug in your Mini Dash Waffle maker and let it heat up.

2. In a small bowl mix the mozzarella cheese, almond flour, baking powder, egg, 1 teaspoon cinnamon, and 1 teaspoon swerve granulated and set aside.
3. In another small bowl, add a tablespoon of butter, 1 teaspoon cinnamon, and 2 teaspoons of swerve confectioners' sweetener.
4. Microwave for 15 seconds and mix well.
5. Spray the waffle maker with nonstick spray and add 1/3 of the batter to your waffle maker. Swirl in 1/3 of the cinnamon, swerve, and butter mixture onto the top of it. Close the waffle maker and let cook for 3-4 minutes.
6. When the first cinnamon roll chaffle is done, make the second and then make the third.
7. While the third chaffle is cooking place 1 tablespoon butter and 1 tablespoon of cream cheese in a small bowl. Heat in the microwave for 10-15 seconds. Start at 10, and if the cream cheese is not soft enough to mix with the butter heat for an additional 5 seconds.
8. Add the vanilla extract, and the swerve confectioner's sweetener to the butter and cream cheese and mix well using a whisk.
9. Drizzle keto cream cheese glaze on top of chaffle.

Nutrition:

(perserving): Calories:180kcal; Carbohydrates:3g; Protein: 7g; Fat:16g; Saturated Fat:9g; Cholesterol:95mg; Sodium:221mg; Potassium:77mg; Fiber: 1g; Sugar: 1g; Vitamin A: 505IU; Calcium: 148mg; Iron: 1mg

Chocolate Chip Chaffle Keto Recipe

Preparation time: 10 minutes

Cooking Time: 8 Minutes

Servings: 2

Ingredients:

- 1 egg
- 1 tbsp heavy whipping cream
- 1/2 tsp coconut flour
- 1 3/4 tsp Lakanto monk fruit golden can use more or less to adjust sweetness
- 1/4 tsp baking powder
- pinch of salt
- 1 tbsp Lily's Chocolate Chips

Directions:

1. Turn on the waffle maker so that it heats up.
2. In a small bowl, combine all ingredients except the chocolate chips and stir well until combined.

3. Grease waffle maker, then pour half of the batter onto the bottom plate of the waffle maker. Sprinkle a few chocolate chips on top and then close.
4. Cook for 3-minutes or until the chocolate chip chaffle dessert is golden brown, then remove from waffle maker with a fork, being careful not to burn your fingers.
5. Repeat with the rest of the batter.
6. Let chaffle sit for a few minutes so that it begins to crisp. If desired, serve with sugar-free whipped topping.

Nutrition:

(per serving): Calories: 146kcal; Carbohydrates: Protein: 6g; Fat: 10g; Saturated Fat:7g; Fiber: 3g; Sugar: 1g

Pumpkin Chocolate Chip Chaffles

Preparation time: 10 minutes

Cooking Time: 12 Minutes

Servings: 2

Ingredients:

- 1/2 cup shredded mozzarella cheese
- 4 teaspoons pumpkin puree
- 1 egg
- 2 tablespoons granulated Swerve
- 1/4 tsp pumpkin pie spice
- 4 teaspoons sugar-free chocolate chips
- 1 tablespoon almond flour

Directions:

1. Plug in your waffle maker.
2. In a small bowl, mix the pumpkin puree and egg. Make sure you mix it well, so all the pumpkin is mixed with the egg.

3. Next, add in the mozzarella cheese, almond flour, swerve and add pumpkin spice and mix well.
4. Then add in your sugar-free chocolate chips
5. Add half the keto pumpkin pie Chaffle mix to the Dish Mini waffle maker at a time. Cook chaffle batter in the waffle maker for 4 minutes.
6. Do not open before the 4 minutes is up. It is very important that you do not open the waffle maker before the 4-minute mark. After that you can open it to check it and make sure it is cooked all the way, but with these chaffles keeping the lid closed the whole time is very important.
7. When the first one is completely done cooking cook the second one.
8. Enjoy with some swerve confectioner's sweetener or whipped cream on top.

Nutrition:

(per serving): Calories: kcal ; Carbohydrates:2g ; Protein: 7g; Fat:7g ; Saturated Fat:3g ; Cholesterol:69mg ; Sodium:138mg ; Potassium: 48mg; Fiber: 1g ; Sugar: 1g ; Vitamin A: 1228IU ; Calcium: 107mg ; Iron: 1mg

Cheesy Garlic Chaffle Bread Recipe

Preparation time: 10 minutes

Cooking Time: 14 Minutes

Servings: 2

Ingredients:

- 1 egg
- 1/2 cup mozzarella cheese, shredded
- 1 tbsp parmesan cheese
- 3/4 tsp coconut flour
- 1/4 tsp baking powder
- 1/8 tsp Italian Seasoning
- Pinch of salt
- 1 tbsp butter, melted
- 1/4 tsp garlic powder
- 1/2 cup mozzarella cheese, shredded
- 1/4 tsp basil seasoning

Directions:

1. Preheat oven to 400 degrees. Plug the Dash Mini Waffle Maker in the wall and allow it to get hot. Lightly grease waffle maker.

2. Combine the first 7 ingredients in a small bowl and stir well to combine.

3. Spoon half of the batter on the waffle maker and close — Cook for 4 minutes or until golden brown.

4. Remove the chaffle bread carefully from the Dash Mini Waffle Maker, then repeat for the rest of the batter.

5. In a small bowl, melt the butter and add garlic powder.

6. Cut each chaffle in half (or thirds), and place on a baking sheet, then brush the tops with the garlic butter mixture.

7. Top with mozzarella cheese and pop in the oven for 4 -5 minutes.

8. Turn oven to broil and move the baking pan to the top shelf for 1-2 minutes so that the cheese begins to bubble and turn golden brown. Watch very carefully, as it can burn quickly on broil. (check every 30 seconds)

9. Remove from oven and sprinkle basil seasoning on top. Enjoy!

Nutrition: (per serving): Calories: 270kcal; Carbohydrates: 3g; Protein:16g; Fat: 21g; Saturated Fat:12g; Fiber: 1g; Sugar: 1g

Best Keto Pizza Chaffle

Preparation time: 10 minutes

Cooking Time: 15 Minutes

Servings: 2

Ingredients:

- 1 tsp coconut flour
- 1 egg white
- 1/2 cup mozzarella cheese, shredded
- `1 tsp cream cheese, softened
- 1/4 tsp baking powder
- 1/8 tsp Italian seasoning
- 1/8 tsp garlic powder
- pinch of salt
- 3 tsp low carb marinara sauce
- 1/2 cup mozzarella cheese
- 6 pepperonis cut in half
- 1 tbsp parmesan cheese, shredded
- 1/4 tsp basil seasoning

Directions:

1. Preheat oven to 400 degrees. Turn waffle maker on or plug it in so that it gets hot.
2. In a small bowl, add coconut flour, egg white, mozzarella cheese, softened cream cheese, baking powder, garlic powder, Italian seasonings, and a pinch of salt.

3. Pour 1/2 of the batter in the waffle maker, close the top, and cook for 4 minutes or until chaffle reaches desired doneness.

4. Carefully remove chaffle from the waffle maker, then follow the same instructions to make the second chaffle.

5. Top each chaffle with tomato sauce (I used 1 1/2 tsp per), pepperoni, mozzarella cheese, and parmesan cheese.

6. Place in the oven on a baking sheet (or straight on the baking rack) on the top shelf of the oven for 5-minutes. Then turn the oven to broil so that the cheese begins to bubble and brown. Keep a close eye as it can burn quickly. I broiled my pizza chaffle for approx 1 min and 30 seconds.

7. Remove from oven and sprinkle basil on top.

8. Enjoy!

Note: The nutritional information provided is for one of the keto Pizza Chaffle so that each person could choose how much they wanted to eat to fit their hunger levels and health goals.

Nutrition:

(per serving): Calories: 241kcal ; Carbohydrates:4g ; Protein:

17g; Fat:18g; SaturatedFat:10g; Cholesterol:49mg; Sodium:430mg; Potassium: 130mg; Fiber: 1g ; Sugar: 1g; VitaminA: 412IU; Calcium:339mg ; Iron: 1mg

Easy Keto Chaffle Sausage Gravy Recipe

Preparation time: 10 minutes

Cooking Time: 10 Minutes

Servings: 2

Ingredients:

For the Chaffle:

- 1 egg
- 1/2 cup mozzarella cheese, grated
- 1 tsp coconut flour
- 1 tsp water
- 1/4 tsp baking powder
- Pinch of salt

For the Keto Sausage Gravy:

- 1/4 cup breakfast sausage, browned
- 3 tbsp chicken broth
- 2 tbsp heavy whipping cream
- 2 tsp cream cheese, softened
- Dash garlic powder

- Pepper to taste
- Dash of onion powder (optional)

Directions:

1. Plug Dash Mini Waffle Maker into the wall and allow it to heat up. Grease lightly or use cooking spray.
2. Combine all the ingredients for the chaffle into a small bowl and stir to combine well.
3. Pour half of the chaffle batter onto the waffle maker, then shut the lid and cook for approximately 4 minutes.
4. Remove chaffle from waffle maker and repeat the same process to make the second chaffle. Set aside to crisp.
5. For the Keto Sausage Gravy:
6. Cook one pound of breakfast sausage and drain. Reserve 1/4 cup for this recipe.

Tip: Make sausage patties out of the rest of the sausage and reserve 1/4 a cup to brown for this recipe. If you aren't familiar with breakfast sausage, it is crumbled like ground beef.

7. Wipe excess grease from the skillet and add 1/4 cup browned breakfast sausage and the rest of the ingredients and bring to a boil stirring continuously.
8. Reduce heat to medium and continue to cook down with the lid off so that it begins to thicken for approx 5-7 minutes. If you'd like it very thick, you can add a bit of

Xanthan Gum, but if you are patient with it simmering, the keto sausage gravy will thicken. Then, it will thicken even more as it cools.

9. Add salt and pepper to taste and spoon keto sausage gravy over chaffles.

10. Enjoy

Nutrition:

(per serving): Calories: 2cal; Carbohydrates:3g; Protein: 11g; Fat:17g; Saturated Fat:10g; Cholesterol:134mg; Sodium:350mg; Potassium:133mg; Fiber: 1g; Sugar: 1g; Vitamin A: 595IU; Vitamin C: 2mg; Calcium: 191mg; Iron: 1mg

Fudgy Chocolate Chaffles

Preparation time: 10 minutes

Cooking Time: 8 Minutes

Ingredients:

- 1 egg
- 2 tbsp mozzarella cheese, shredded
- 2 tbsp cocoa
- 2 tbsp Lakanto monk fruit powdered
- 1 tsp coconut flour
- 1 tsp heavy whipping cream
- 1/4 tsp baking powder
- 1/4 tsp vanilla extract
- pinch of salt

Directions:

1. Turn on waffle or chaffle maker. I use the Dash Mini Waffle Maker. Grease lightly or use a cooking spray.
2. In a small bowl, combine all ingredients.
3. Cover the dash mini waffle maker with 1/2 of the batter. Close the mini waffle maker and cook for 4 minutes.

Remove the chaffle from the waffle maker carefully as it is very hot.

4. Repeat the steps above.
5. Serve with sugar-free strawberry ice cream or sugar-free whipped topping.

Note: The nutritional information does not include the Lakanto Monk fruit powdered sugar as most subtract to calculate net carbs. The nutritional info is based on one chaffle per serving.

The nutritional information is provided for the fudgy chocolate chaffle recipe only.

Nutrition:

(per serving): Calories: 10cal ; Carbohydrates:5g ; Protein: 7g; Fat:7g ; Saturated Fat:4g ; Cholesterol:97mg ; Sodium:132mg ; Potassium: 176mg; Fiber: 3g ; Sugar: 1g ; Vitamin A: 255IU ; Calcium: 121mg ; Iron: 1mg

Mouthwatering Blueberry Chaffles

Preparation time: 10 minutes

Cooking Time: 8 Minutes

Servings: 2

Ingredients:

- 1 egg
- 1/3 cup mozzarella cheese, shredded
- 1 tbsp blueberries
- 1 tsp cream cheese
- 1 tsp coconut flour
- 1/4 tsp baking powder
- 1/4 tsp vanilla extract
- 2 squirts liquid Pure Sweetener (can substitute 3/4 tsp other sweeteners such as Monk fruit powdered)
- 1/4 tsp cinnamon
- Pinch of salt

Directions:

1. Turn on waffle or chaffle maker. Grease lightly or use a cooking spray.
2. In a small bowl, combine all ingredients except the blueberries
3. Cover the dash mini waffle maker with 1/2 of the batter then sprinkle a couple of blueberries on top. Close the mini waffle maker and cook for 4 minutes. Remove the chaffle from the waffle maker carefully,
4. Repeat the steps above.
5. Serve with sugar-free maple syrup, whipped cream, or keto ice cream.

Nutrition:

(per serving): Calories: 113kcal ; Carbohydrates:3g ; Protein:

7g; Fat: 7g; Saturated Fat:4g; Cholesterol:99mg ; Sodium:1mg ; Potassium:93mg ; Fiber: 1g ; Sugar: 1g ; Vitamin A: 278IU ; Vitamin C: 1mg ; Calcium:134mg ;Iron: 1mg

Open-faced French Dip Keto Chaffle Sandwich

Preparation time: 10 minutes

Cooking Time: 12 Minutes

Servings: 2

Ingredients:

- 1 egg white
- 1/4 cup mozzarella cheese, shredded (packed)
- 1/4 cup sharp cheddar cheese, shredded (packed)
- 3/4 tsp water
- 1 tsp coconut flour
- 1/4 tsp baking powder
- Pinch of salt

Directions:

1. Preheat oven to 425 degrees. Plug the Dash Mini Waffle Maker in the wall and grease lightly once it is hot.
2. Combine all of the ingredients in a bowl and stir to combine.
3. Spoon out 1/2 of the batter on the waffle maker and close lid. Set a timer for 4 minutes and do not lift the lid until the cooking time is complete. Lifting beforehand can cause the Chaffle keto sandwich recipe to separate and

stick to the waffle iron. You have to let it cook the entire 4 minutes before lifting the lid.

4. Remove the chaffle from the waffle iron and set aside. Repeat the same steps above with the rest of the chaffle batter.
5. Cover a cookie sheet with parchment paper and place chaffles a few inches apart.
6. Add 1/4 to 1/3 cup of the slow cooker keto roast beef from the following recipe. Make sure to drain the excess broth/gravy before adding to the top of the chaffle.
7. Add a slice of deli cheese or shredded cheese on top. Swiss and provolone are both great options.
8. Place on the top rack of the oven for 5 minutes so that the cheese can melt. If you'd like the cheese to bubble and begin to brown, turn oven to broil for 1 min. (The swiss cheese may not brown)
9. Enjoy open-faced with a small bowl of beef broth for dipping.

Note: The nutritional information provided is only for the chaffles sandwich keto recipe. It does not include the beef or added cheese on top of the sandwich. That info will vary depending on the cut of beef you use and type of cheese.

Nutrition:

(per serving): Calories: 118kcal; Carbohydrates:2g; Fiber: 1g; Protein: 9g; Fat: 8g

Keto Chaffle Taco Shells

Servings: 5

Cooking Time: 20 Minutes

Ingredients:

- 1 tablespoon almond flour
- 1 cup taco blend cheese
- 2 eggs
- 1/4 tsp taco seasoning

Directions:

1. In a bowl, mix almond flour, taco blend cheese, eggs, and taco seasoning. I find it easiest to mix everything using a fork.
2. Add 1.5 tablespoons of taco chaffle batter to the waffle maker at a time — Cook chaffle batter in the waffle maker for 4 minutes.
3. Remove the taco chaffle shell from the waffle maker and drape over the side of a bowl. I used my pie pan because it was what I had on hand, but just about any bowl will work.

4. Continue making chaffle taco shells until you are out of batter. Then fill your taco shells with taco meat, your favorite toppings, and enjoy!

Nutrition:

(per serving): Calories: 113kcal; Carbohydrates:1g; Protein: 8g; Fat:9g; Saturated Fat:4g; Cholesterol:87mg; Sodium:181mg; Potassium:43mg; Fiber: 1g; Sugar: 1g ; Vitamin A: 243IU ; Calcium: 160mg; Iron: 1mg

Peanut Butter Chocolate Chip Chaffle

Preparation time: 10 minutes

Cooking Time: 8 Minutes

Servings: 2

Ingredients:

- 1 egg.
- 1/4 cup shredded mozzarella cheese
- 2 tablespoons creamy Peanut Butter.
- 1 tablespoon Almond Flour.
- 1 tablespoon Granulated Swerve.
- 1 teaspoon Vanilla extract.
- 1 tablespoon low carb chocolate chips.

Directions:

1. Plug in your waffle maker.
2. In a small bowl, mix the peanut butter and egg. Make sure you mix it well, so all the peanut butter is mixed with the egg.

3. Next, add in the mozzarella cheese, almond flour, swerve and chocolate chips and mix well.
4. Add half the keto peanut butter chocolate chip Chaffle mix to the Dish Mini waffle maker at a time. Cook chaffle batter in the waffle maker for minutes.
5. When the first one is completely done cooking cook the second one.
6. Enjoy with some swerve confectioner's sweetener or whipped cream on top.

Nutrition:

(per serving): Calories: 193kcal ; Carbohydrates:5g ; Protein:

11g; Fat:15g; SaturatedFat:4g; Cholesterol:93mg; Sodium:193mg

; Potassium: 134mg; Fiber: 1g ; Sugar: 2g ; Vitamin A: 213IU ; Calcium: 9g; Iron: 1mg

Mini Keto Pizza Chaffle Recipe

Preparation time: 10 minutes

Cooking Time: 10 Minutes

Servings: 2

Ingredients:

- 1/2 cup Shredded Mozzarella cheese
- 1 tablespoon almond flour
- 1/2 tsp baking powder
- 1 egg
- 1/4 tsp garlic powder
- 1/4 tsp basil
- 2 tablespoons low carb pasta sauce
- 2 tablespoons mozzarella cheese

Directions:

1. While the waffle maker is heating up, in a bowl mix mozzarella cheese, baking powder, garlic, basil, egg, and almond flour.
2. Pour 1/the mixture into your mini waffle maker.

3. Cook for 5 minutes until your pizza waffle is completely cooked. If you check it and the waffle sticks to the waffle maker, let it cook for another minute or two.
4. Next, put the remainder of the pizza crust mix into the waffle maker and cook it.
5. Once both pizza crusts are cooked, place them on the baking sheet of your toaster oven.
6. Put 1 tablespoon of low carb pasta sauce on top of each pizza crust.
7. Sprinkle 1 tablespoon of shredded mozzarella cheese on top of each one.
8. Bake at 350 degrees in the toaster oven for roughly 5 minutes, just until the cheese is melted.

Nutrition:

(per serving): Calories: 1kcal; Carbohydrates:4g; Protein: 13g; Fat:14g; Saturated Fat:6g; Cholesterol:116mg; Sodium:301mg; Potassium:178mg; Fiber: 1g; Sugar: 1g; Vitamin A: 408IU; Calcium: 290mg; Iron: 1mg

Maple Pumpkin Keto Chaffle Recipe

Preparation time: 10 minutes

Cooking Time: 16 Minutes

Servings: 2

Ingredients:

- 2 eggs
- 3/4 tsp baking powder
- 2 tsp pumpkin puree (100% pumpkin)
- 3/4 tsp pumpkin pie spice
- 4 tsp heavy whipping cream
- 2 tsp Lakanto Sugar-Free Maple Syrup
- 1 tsp coconut flour

- 1/2 cup mozzarella cheese, shredded
- 1/2 tsp vanilla
- Pinch of salt

Directions:

1. Turn on chaffle maker.
2. In a small bowl, combine all ingredients.
3. Cover the dash mini waffle maker with 1/4 of the batter and cook for 4 minutes.
4. Repeat 3 more times until you have made Maple Syrup Pumpkin Keto Waffles (Chaffles).
5. Serve with sugar-free maple syrup or keto ice cream.

Nutrition: (perserving): Calories:201kcal; Carbohydrates:4g; Protein:12g; Fat:15g; Saturated Fat:8g; Cholesterol:200mg; Sodium:249mg; Potassium:271mg; Fiber: 1g; Sugar: 1g; Vitamin A: 1341IU; Calcium: 254mg; Iron: 1mg

Garlic Bread Chaffles

Preparation time: 10 minutes

Cooking Time: 11 Minutes

Servings: 2

Ingredients:

- 1/2 cup shredded Mozzarella cheese
- 1 egg
- 1/2 tsp basil
- 1/4 tsp garlic powder
- 1 tbsp almond flour
- 1 tbsp butter
- 1/4 tsp garlic powder
- 1/4 cup shredded mozzarella cheese

Directions:

1. Heat up your Dash mini waffle maker.
2. In a small bowl, mix the egg, 1/tsp basil, 1/4 tsp garlic powder, 1 tablespoon almond flour and 1/2 cup Mozzarella Cheese.

3. Add 1/2 of the batter into your mini waffle maker and cook for 4 minutes. If they are still a bit uncooked, leave it cooking for another 2 minutes. Then cook the rest of the batter to make a second chaffle.
4. In a small bowl, add 1 tablespoon butter and 1/tsp garlic powder and melt in the microwave. It will take about 25 seconds or so, depending on your microwave.
5. Place the chaffles on a baking sheet and use a rubber brush to spread the butter and garlic mixture on top.
6. Add 1/8th a cup of cheese on top of each chaffle.
7. Put chaffles in the oven or a toaster oven at 400 degrees and cook until the cheese is melted.

Nutrition:

(per serving): Calories: 231kcal ; Carbohydrates:2g ; Protein: 13g; Fat:19g; Saturated Fat:10g; Cholesterol:130mg; Sodium:346mg; Potassium: 52mg ; Fiber: 1g; Sugar: 1g ; Vitamin A: 5IU ; Calcium: 232mg; Iron: 1mg

Basic Keto Low Carb Chaffle Recipe

Preparation time: 10 minutes

Cooking Time: 8 Minutes

Servings: 2

Ingredients:

- 1 egg
- 1/2 cup cheddar cheese, shredded

Directions:

1. Turn waffle maker on or plug it in so that it heats and grease both sides.
2. In a small bowl, crack an egg, then add the 1/cup cheddar cheese and stir to combine.
3. Pour 1/2 of the batter in the waffle maker and close the top.
4. Cook for 3-minutes or until it reaches desired doneness.
5. Carefully remove from waffle maker and set aside for 2-3 minutes to give it time to crisp.

6. Follow the instructions again to make the second chaffle.

Nutrition:

(per serving): Calories: 291kcal; Carbohydrates:1g; Protein: 20g; Fat:23g; Saturated Fat:13g; Cholesterol:223mg; Sodium:413mg; Potassium: 116mg; Sugar:1g; Vitamin A: 804IU; Calcium: 432mg; Iron: 1mg

Keto Protein Chaffle

Preparation time: 5 minutes

Cooking Time: 8 Minutes

Servings: 2

Ingredients:

- 1 egg (beaten)
- ½ cup whey protein powder
- A pinch of salt
- 1 tsp baking powder
- 3 tbsp sour cream
- ½ tsp vanilla extract

Topping:

- 2 tbsp heavy cream
- 1 tbsp granulated swerve

Directions:

1. Plug the waffle maker to preheat it and spray it with a non-stick cooking spray.
2. In a mixing bowl, whisk together the egg, vanilla and sour cream.
3. In another mixing bowl, combine the protein powder, baking powder and salt.
4. Pour the flour mixture into the egg mixture and mix until the ingredients are well combined and you form a smooth batter.
5. Pour an appropriate amount of the batter into the waffle maker and spread the batter to the edges to cover all the holes on the waffle maker.
6. Close the waffle maker and cook for about 4 minutes or according to your waffle maker's settings.
7. After the cooking cycle, use a plastic or silicone utensil to remove the chaffle from the waffle iron.
8. Repeat step 4 to 6 until you have cooked all the batter into chaffles.
9. For the topping, whisk together the cream and swerve in a mixing bowl until smooth and fluffy.
10. Top the chaffles with the cream and enjoy.

Nutrition: Fat 25.9g 33% Carbohydrate 13.1g 5% Sugars 2.1g Protein 41.6g

Garlic Mayo Vegan Chaffles

Preparation time: 8 minutes

Servings:2

Cooking Time:5minutes

Ingredients:

- 1 tbsp. chia seeds
- 2 ½ tbsps. water
- ¼ cup low carb vegan cheese
- 2 tbsps. coconut flour
- 1 cup low carb vegan cream cheese, softened
- 1 tsp. garlic powder
- pinch of salt
- 2 tbsps. vegan garlic mayo for topping

Directions:

1. Preheat your square waffle maker.
2. In a small bowl, mix chia seeds and water, let it stand for 5 minutes Utes.
3. Add all ingredients to the chia seeds mixture and mix well.

4. Pour vegan chaffle batter in a greased waffle maker
5. Close the waffle maker and cook for about 3-minutesutes.
6. Once chaffles are cooked, remove from the maker.
7. Top with garlic mayo and pepper.
8. Enjoy!

Nutrition:

Protein: 32% 42 kcal Fat: 63% 82 kcal Carbohydrates: 5% 6 kcal

Broccoli Chaffle

Preparation time: 10 minutes

Servings:4

Cooking Time:15 Minutes

Ingredients:

Batter

- 4 eggs
- 2 cups grated mozzarella cheese
- 1 cup steamed broccoli, chopped
- Salt and pepper to taste
- 1 clove garlic, minced
- 1 teaspoon chili flakes
- 2 tablespoons almond flour
- 2 teaspoons baking powder

Other

- 2 tablespoons cooking spray to brush the waffle maker
- ¼ cup mascarpone cheese for serving

Directions:

1. Preheat the waffle maker.
2. Add the eggs, grated mozzarella, chopped broccoli, salt and pepper, minced garlic, chili flakes, almond flour and baking powder to a bowl.
3. Mix with a fork.
4. Brush the heated waffle maker with cooking spray and add a few tablespoons of the batter.
5. Close the lid and cook for about 7 minutes depending on your waffle maker.
6. Serve each chaffle with mascarpone cheese.

Nutrition:

Calories 229, fat 15 g, carbs 6 g, sugar 1.1 g, Protein 13.1 g, sodium 194 mg

Celery and Cottage Cheese Chaffle

Preparation time: 9 minutes

Servings:4

Cooking Time:15 Minutes

Ingredients:

Batter

- 4 eggs
- 2 cups grated cheddar cheese
- 1 cup fresh celery, chopped
- Salt and pepper to taste
- 2 tablespoons chopped almonds
- 2 teaspoons baking powder

Other

- 2 tablespoons cooking spray to brush the waffle maker
- ¼ cup cottage cheese for serving

Directions:

1. Preheat the waffle maker.

2. Add the eggs, grated mozzarella cheese, chopped celery, salt and pepper, chopped almonds and baking powder to a bowl.

3. Mix with a fork.

4. Brush the heated waffle maker with cooking spray and add a few tablespoons of the batter.

5. Close the lid and cook for about 7 minutes depending on your waffle maker.

6. Serve each chaffle with cottage cheese on top.

Nutrition:

Calories 385, fat 31.6 g, carbs 4 g, sugar 1.5 g, Protein 22.2 g, sodium 492 mg

Lettuce Chaffle Sandwich

Preparation time: 9 minutes

Cooking Time: 5 Minutes

Servings: 2

Ingredients:

- 1 large egg
- 1 tbsp. almond flour
- 1 tbsp. full-fat Greek yogurt
- 1/8 tsp baking powder
- 1/4 cup shredded Swiss cheese
- 4 lettuce leaves

Directions:

1. Switch on your minutes waffle maker.
2. Grease it with cooking spray.
3. Mix together egg, almond flour, yogurts, baking powder and cheese in mixing bowl.
4. Pour 1/2 cup of the batter into the center of your waffle iron and close the lid.

5. Cook chaffles for about 2-3 minutes Utes until cooked through.
6. Repeat with remaining batter
7. Once cooked, carefully transfer to plate. Serve lettuce leaves between 2 chaffles.
8. Enjoy!

Nutrition:

Protein: 22% 40 kcal Fat: 66% 120 kcal Carbohydrates: 12% 22 kcal

Cocoa Chaffles With Coconut Cream

Preparation time: 9 minutes

Cooking Time: 5 Minutes

Servings: 2

Ingredients:

- 1 egg
- 1/2 cup mozzarella cheese
- 1 tsp stevia
- 1 tsp vanilla
- 2 tbsps. almond flour
- 1 tbsp. sugar-free chocolate chips
- 2 tbsps. cocoa powder

TOPPING

- 1 scoop coconut cream
- 1 tbsp. coconut flour

Directions:

1. Mix together chaffle ingredients in a bowl and mix well.
2. Preheat your dash minutes waffle maker. Spray waffle maker with cooking spray.
3. Pour 1/2 batter into the minutes-waffle maker and close the lid.
4. Cook chaffles for about 2-minutesutes and remove from the maker.
5. Make chaffles from the rest of the batter.
6. Serve with a scoop of coconut cream between two chaffles.
7. Drizzle coconut flour on top.
8. Enjoy with afternoon coffee!

Nutrition:

Protein: 26% 60 kcal Fat: 65% 152 kcal Carbohydrates: 21 kcal

Shrimp Avocado Chaffle Sandwich

Preparation time: 8 minutes

Cooking Time: 32 Minutes

Servings: 2

Ingredients:

- 2 cups shredded mozzarella cheese
- 4 large eggs
- ½ tsp curry powder
- ½ tsp oregano

Shrimp Sandwich Filling:

- 1-pound raw shrimp (peeled and deveined)
- 1 large avocado (diced)
- 4 slices cooked bacon
- 2 tbsp sour cream
- ½ tsp paprika
- 1 tsp Cajun seasoning
- 1 tbsp olive oil
- ¼ cup onion (finely chopped)

- 1 red bell pepper (diced)

Directions:

1. Plug the waffle maker to preheat it and spray it with a non-stick cooking spray.
2. Break the eggs into a mixing bowl and beat. Add the cheese, oregano and curry. Mix until the ingredients are well combined.
3. Pour an appropriate amount of the batter into the waffle maker and spread out the batter to the edges to cover all the holes on the waffle maker. This should make 8 mini waffles.
4. Close the waffle maker and cook for about minutes or according to your waffle maker's settings.
5. After the cooking cycle, use a silicone or plastic utensil to remove the chaffle from the waffle maker.
6. Repeat step 3 to 5 until you have cooked all the batter into chaffles.
7. Heat up the olive oil in a large skillet over medium to high heat.
8. Add the shrimp and cook until the shrimp is pink and tender.
9. Remove the skillet from heat and use a slotted spoon to transfer the shrimp to a paper towel lined plate to drain for a few minutes.

10. Put the shrimp in a mixing bowl. Add paprika and Cajun seasoning. Toss until the shrimps are all coated with seasoning.

11. To assemble the sandwich, place one chaffle on a flat surface and spread some sour cream over it. Layer some shrimp, onion, avocado, diced pepper and one slice of bacon over it. Cover with another chaffle.

12. Repeat step 10 until you have assembled all the ingredients into sandwiches.

13. Serve and enjoy.

Nutrition:

Fat 32.1g 41% Carbohydrate 10.8g 4% Sugars 2.5g Protein 44.8g

Cuban Pork Sandwich

Preparation time: 5 minutes

Cooking Time: 10 Minutes

Servings: 2

Ingredients:

Sandwich Filling:

- 25 g swiss cheese (sliced)
- 2 ounces cooked deli ham (thinly sliced)
- 3 slices pickle chips
- ½ tbsp Dijon mustard
- ½ tbsp mayonnaise
- 3 ounces pork roast
- 1 tsp paprika
- 1 stalk celery (diced)

Chaffle:

- 1 tsp baking powder
- 1 large egg (beaten)
- 1 tbsp full-fat Greek yogurt
- 4 tbsp mozzarella cheese
- 1 tbsp almond flour

Directions:

1. Preheat the oven to 350°F and grease a baking sheet.
2. Plug the waffle maker to preheat it and spray it with a non-stick cooking spray.

3. In a mixing bowl, combine the almond flour, cheese and baking powder.
4. Add the egg and yogurt. Mix until the ingredients are well combined.
5. Fill the waffle maker with an appropriate amount of the batter and spread the batter to the edges to cover all the holes on the waffle maker.
6. Close the waffle maker and cook the waffle until it is crispy. That will take about 5 minutes. The time may vary in some waffle makers.7. After the cooking cycle, remove the chaffle from the waffle maker with a plastic or silicone utensil.
7. Repeat step 4 to 6 until you have cooked all the batter into chaffles.
8. In a small mixing bowl, combine the mustard, oregano and mayonnaise.
9. Brush the mustard-mayonnaise mixture over the surface of both chaffles.
10. Layer the pork, ham, pickles and celery over one of the chaffles. Layer the cheese slices on top and cover it with the second chaffle.
11. Place it on the baking sheet. Place it in oven and bake until the cheese melts. You can place a heavy stainless place over the chaffle to make the sandwich come out flat after baking
12. After the baking cycle, remove the chaffle sandwich from the oven and let it cool for a few minutes.
13. Serve warm and enjoy.

Nutrition:

Fat 52.3g 67% Carbohydrate 17.3g 6% Sugars 2.7g Protein 82.6g

Keto Chocolate Chaffles

Preparation time: 9 minutes

Cooking Time: 8 Minutes

Servings: 2

Ingredients:

- 1 tsp swerve
- 1 large egg
- 2 tbsp cream cheese
- 1 tbsp unsweetened cocoa powder
- 2 tbsp almond flour
- 1/4 tsp baking powder
- 1 tsp vanilla extract

Topping:

- 1 tbsp granulated swerve
- ¼ tsp vanilla extract
- ¼ tsp cinnamon
- 2 tbsp cream cheese (softened)

Directions:

1. Plug the waffle maker and preheat it. Spray it with non-stick spray.
2. In a large mixing bowl, combine the almond flour, stevia extract, baking powder and cocoa powder.
3. Add the eggs, cream cheese and vanilla extract. Mix until the ingredients are well combined and you have formed a smooth batter.
4. Fill the waffle maker with the batter. Spread out the batter to cover all the holes on the waffle maker.
5. Close the lid of the waffle maker and bake for about 4 minutes or until the chaffle is crispy.
6. After the cooking cycle, remove the chaffle from the iron using a plastic or silicone utensil and set aside.
7. Repeat step 4 to 5 until you have cooked all the batter into waffles.
8. Leave the batter to cool completely.
9. Meanwhile, prepare the topping. Combine the cream cheese, vanilla extract, cinnamon and swerve in a mixing bowl and mix until smooth.
10. Top chaffles with the cream cheese mixture and enjoy.

Nutrition: Fat 23.8g31% Carbohydrate 10.1g4% Sugars 1.6gProtein 2g

Tuna Salad Chaffles

Preparation time: 9 minutes

Cooking Time: 8 Minutes

Servings: 2

Ingredients:

Tuna Sandwich:

- 1 can water packed tuna (drained)
- 1 small sweet onion (chopped)
- 1 green bell pepper (finely chopped)
- 1 small carrot (peeled and chopped)
- 2 tbsp mayonnaise
- ½ tsp paprika
- ¼ tsp ground black pepper or to taste
- ¼ tsp salt or to taste
- 1 celery stalk (chopped)
- 1 tbsp freshly chopped parsley

Chaffle:

- 2 eggs (beaten)
- 4 tbsp almond flour
- 1 cup shredded mozzarella cheese
- ¾ tsp baking powder
- ½ tsp garlic powder

Directions:

1. Plug the waffle maker to preheat it and spray the it with a non-stick cooking spray.
2. In a mixing bowl, combine the almond flour, baking powder, garlic powder and mozzarella. Add the eggs and mix until the ingredients are well combined.
3. Fill the waffle maker with an appropriate amount of the batter and spread the batter to the edges to cover all the holes on the waffle maker.
4. Close the waffle maker and cook for about minutes or according to waffle maker's settings.
5. After the cooking cycle, use a silicone or plastic utensil to remove the chaffle from the waffle maker.
6. Repeat step 3 to 5 until you have cooked all the batter into chaffles.
7. In a mixing bowl, combine the tuna, celery, pepper, onion, salt, paprika, carrot, onion and green pepper. Add the mayonnaise and toss until the ingredients are well combined.
8. Place one of the chaffle of a flat surface and spoon ½ of the tuna salad into it. Top with fresh parsley. Cover it with another chaffle and press.
9. Repeat step 8 to make the second sandwich.
10. Serve and enjoy.

Nutrition:

Fat 26.3g 34% Carbohydrate 19.6g 7% Sugars 7.7g Protein 37.8g

Keto Pizza Chaffle

Preparation time: 9 minutes

Cooking Time: 15 Minutes

Servings: 2

Ingredients:

Pizza Filing:

- 1/3 cups pepperoni slices
- 1 tbsp marinara sauce
- ½ cup shredded mozzarella cheese
- 1 onion (finely chopped)
- 1 small green bell pepper (finely chopped)

Chaffle:

- 1 egg (beaten)
- A pinch of Italian seasoning
- A pinch of salt
- ½ cup mozzarella cheese
- ¼ tsp baking powder
- ½ tsp dried basil
- A pinch of garlic powder
- 1 tbsp + 1 tsp almond flour

Directions:

1. Preheat the oven to 400°F and line a baking sheet with parchment paper.

2. Plug the waffle maker and preheat it. Spray it with a nonstick spray.
3. For the chaffle: In a mixing bowl, combine the baking powder, almond flour, garlic powder, Italian seasoning, basil, mozzarella cheese and salt. Add the egg and mix until the ingredients are well combined.
4. Fill the waffle maker with appropriate amount of the batter and spread the batter to the edges of the waffle maker to cover all the holes on the waffle maker.
5. Close the lid of the waffle maker and cook for about minutes or according to waffle maker's settings.
6. After the baking cycle, remove the chaffle from waffle maker with a silicone or plastic utensil.
7. Repeat step 4 to 6 until you have cooked all the batter into chaffles.
8. Top each of the chaffles with the marinara sauce, sprinkle the finely chopped onions and pepper over the chaffles.
9. Top with shredded mozzarella cheese and layer the pepperoni slices on the cheese topping.
10. Gently place the chaffles on the lined baking sheet. Place the baking sheet in the oven and bake for about 5 minutes. Afterwards, broil for about 1 minute.
11. Remove the pizza chaffles from the oven and let them cook for a few minutes.
12. Serve warm and enjoy.

Nutrition:

Fat 23.2g 30% Carbohydrate 14.9g 5% Sugars 6.8g Protein 16.8g

Lightning Source UK Ltd.
Milton Keynes UK
UKHW020640060521
383241UK00015B/1147